Short Stack Editions | Volume 11

by Andrea Albin

Short Stack Editions

Publisher: Nick Fauchald
Creative Director: Rotem Raffe
Editor: Kaitlyn Goalen
Copy Editor: Abby Tannenbaum
Business Manager: Mackenzie Smith

ISBN 978-0-9907853-0-9

Printed in New York City
September 2014

Table of Contents

Savory

Sweet

Drinks

Most ingredients gain their devotees through recipes. But not apples, which seduce us long before they enter our kitchens.

From the time we're young, the fruit is embedded into our eating consciousness through myths, literature, maxims and the brown-bag lunch. They are enshrined as a snack, eaten raw out of hand.

Given their cultural weight and widespread accessibility, it's surprising that apples aren't even more of a cooking muse. Apple pie aside, the fruit sees a fraction of the excitement that is afforded to other crops. It's almost as if all that early exposure we receive evaporates to tedium in the kitchen.

Enter Andrea Albin, who has allowed the apple's role in her kitchen to mature past juice boxes and fairy tales. In some of her recipes, apples are the cutting edge, serving as spicy pickles in a *banh mi* sandwich or the crown jewel of a tahini-slicked tart. Other recipes acknowledge our nostalgia, but still enliven the format: Her apple pie is spiced with pink peppercorns, and applesauce is spiked with Calvados to form a complex, boozy dessert.

Every recipe we cooked from this edition felt like rediscovering an old flame: hauntingly familiar but carrying the excitement of the new.

We hope that the reunion is just as sweet for you.

—*The Editors*

Introduction

The apple needs no introduction. Its enticing perfection has held sway over our imaginations forever. Impeccably beautiful, apples call to us like sirens from the tree and supermarket aisle alike. Their alluring nature is well documented in literature; Eve and Snow White had no power against them. As Americans, we begin our love affair with the fruit as young children. I remember reading about Johnny Appleseed in my second-grade class and feeling proud to have an apple in my lunchbox that day.

Few things excite me more than those first few gusts of crisp fall air that signal the beginning of apple season, and that's been the case for as long as I can remember. One of my fondest and earliest food memories is the smell of apples cooking in sweet butter for my mother's paper-thin apple tarts. And to this day, the taste of apple butter sends me into nostalgic reveries for the two years my family lived in Lancaster, Pennsylvania, where we bought fresh apple butter from the Amish market every Saturday. In addition, the Thanksgiving stuffing (which must be America's most treasured comfort food) my family favors prominently features apples. (You'll find my updated versions of these childhood favorites in this book.)

The beauty of apples is that they come in countless varieties, each offering different flavors, textures and nuances. Some, such as the Fuji, have a great crunch and delicate perfume that make it best for eating raw. Others, like the Macintosh, are a bit too mealy for eating out of hand, but cook down into the most luxurious applesauce. Amazingly, most varieties are versatile workhorses that shine in all preparations. Served raw, they add crunch, acidity, sweetness and juiciness to their companions. When cooked, they can retain their crispness and personality, morph into tender caramelized morsels or melt into a thick, luscious puree. Best of all, apples lend themselves equally well to both sweet and savory preparations; they are as comfortable next to a pork chop as they are in a pie.

In this cookbook, I share recipes that celebrate apples in all their incarnations and in every part of the meal, from appetizers to side dishes, drinks, main courses and, of course, desserts. You'll find inspired combinations like apple and smoked trout in an easy-but-impressive spread for crostini; innovative applications, as in the Farro Pilaf (p. 19) and Barbecue Chicken (p. 26); and updated classics such as the Cheddar-Crusted Apple Pie (p. 40) and a Calvados Applesauce (p. 32) rich enough to hold its own as dessert.

Please enjoy these recipes and explore the delicious versatility of the amazing apple—not just this autumn, but also throughout the year.

—*Andrea Albin*

Recipes

A Note About Choosing Apples

Selecting apples for cooking is largely a matter of preference. In my testing, I found that the majority of apples worked well in both raw and cooked preparations, but where they lie on the sweet-tart spectrum varies and depends on individual taste. There are, however, a few varieties—namely Fuji and Honeycrisp—that are best eaten only raw because of their excellent, crisp texture and the fact that their subtle aromas don't hold up as well as other varieties during cooking. Conversely, there are a few varieties, including Macintosh, Rome and Empire, that have less-appealing textures when raw and really benefit from cooking. There are just too many apples available these days to go into the specific flavor profiles of each, but I've indicated a variety or two of my preferred apples in each recipe. Depending on your taste and what's available at your local market, feel free to experiment.

Smoked-Trout Spread

The complex flavors of this knockout appetizer belie the ease of its preparation. Smoked trout is one of my all-time favorite ingredients and it's ready to use straight out of the package. Here, the sour cream quells the smokiness of the trout, while the crisp, tartness of the apple adds crunch and much-needed brightness. I like to serve this as a dip with crostini before dinner, but the leftovers also make an excellent addition to your bagel breakfast the next morning.

¼ cup sour cream

¼ cup mayonnaise

1 medium shallot, minced

Zest and juice of 1 lemon

1 tablespoon prepared horseradish

8 ounces smoked trout, skin and bones removed

1 tart, crisp apple, such as Granny Smith, cored and cut into ¼-inch dice

2 tablespoons finely chopped chives

Freshly ground black pepper

Hot paprika, for garnish

1 small baguette, sliced and toasted

serves
·6·

Combine the sour cream, mayonnaise, shallot, lemon juice and zest and horseradish in a medium bowl. Flake the trout into the bowl and mix to combine thoroughly. Stir in the apple and chives and season to taste with pepper.

Transfer the spread to a serving bowl, cover and refrigerate for at least 1 hour or up to overnight. Dust with paprika and serve with the toasted baguette.

Grilled-Apple Pintxos with Ham and Cheese

Pintxos are the Basque equivalent of tapas—small appetizers meant to be enjoyed with a predinner drink—and often come neatly packaged on toothpicks or little skewers. Here, caramelized grilled apple slices stand in for the more traditional quince paste. These one-bite hors d'oeuvres are excellent alongside a dry cava or other sparkling wine.

2 sweet, crisp apples, such as Pink Lady, cored and cut into 12 wedges each

⅓ cup sugar in the raw

1 teaspoon rosemary leaves

8 ounces Manchego cheese, rinds removed and cut into 24 ¼-inch-thick rectangles

24 thin slices Serrano ham (about 8 ounces)

makes ·24·

Preheat an outdoor grill to medium heat. Toss the apples with the sugar and rosemary in a bowl. Place a double layer of foil on the grill and arrange the apples on top in a single layer. Cook, flipping the apples halfway through, until they're caramelized and tender, about 16 minutes.

Let the apples cool to room temperature. Skewer each apple wedge onto a toothpick with a slice of Manchego and a slice of ham. Arrange on a platter and serve.

Chicken & Apple Meatballs with Agrodolce

Like perfectly matched dance partners, the chicken and apple in these meatballs work in harmony, neither overpowering nor outshining the other; instead, their coupling produces an understated, graceful and elegant result. Grinding chicken thighs in a food processor instead of using preground chicken ensures that the meat stays moist and flavorful. The agrodolce, an Italian condiment that means "sweet and sour," plays up those same sweet and sour notes in the apple.

1 pound boneless, skinless chicken thighs, cut into 1-inch pieces (do not trim fat)

2 tablespoons extra-virgin olive oil

½ small onion, finely chopped

1 small garlic clove, minced

2 small cooking apples, such as Empire, peeled and cut into ¼-inch dice

1 teaspoon chopped fresh thyme

Kosher salt and freshly ground black pepper

¾ cup cubed stale baguette or crusty Italian bread

¼ cup whole milk

1 large egg, lightly beaten

2 tablespoons tomato paste

¼ cup apple cider vinegar

⅓ cup light brown sugar

½ cup chicken broth

Steamed rice, for serving (optional)

serves
-8-

To make the chicken easier to grind, place it in a bowl or resealable plastic bag and freeze until firm, but not frozen through, about 45 minutes. Meanwhile, heat the oil in a large skillet over medium heat. Add the onion and garlic and cook, stirring occasionally, until slightly softened, about 3 minutes. Add the apples, thyme and ½ teaspoon of salt and continue to cook until the apples are tender and golden, about 5 minutes more; let cool slightly in the pan.

Coarsely grind the bread in the food processor and transfer it to a large bowl. Add the milk to the bowl and let stand for 10 minutes. Transfer the chicken to the food processor and pulse until most of the chicken is finely ground but there are some small (about ¼ inch) pieces remaining. Add the ground chicken, apple mixture, egg, ¾ teaspoon of salt and a few grinds of pepper to the bowl along with the bread crumbs. Mix with your hands to combine thoroughly.

Roll the mixture into approximately 24 one-inch balls and place them in a 9-by-13-inch baking dish. Cover and refrigerate for at least 1 hour and up to overnight.

Preheat the oven to 425°. Remove the meatballs from the refrigerator and let them sit at room temperature for 20 minutes. Make the agrodolce by whisking together the tomato paste, cider vinegar, sugar and chicken broth in a small bowl. Bake the meatballs for 10 minutes, then add the agrodolce and continue baking for 10 minutes longer. Switch the oven to broil and broil the meatballs about 3 inches from the element until lightly browned, 3 to 5 minutes.

If you're serving the meatballs as an appetizer, skewer them with toothpicks, arrange on a platter and drizzle with additional agrodolce. Otherwise, serve over rice.

Apple & Fennel Salad with Bacon-Buttermilk Dressing

The buttermilk dressing that coats this salad is a favorite recipe of mine. Creamy and tart, with a hint of garlic, it is essentially ranch dressing for grown-ups. I like it best on salads with lots of crunch like this one, and the tangy buttermilk works beautifully with the apples and the fennel's herbal complexity. Add some homemade bacon bits and you have a gorgeous, satisfying salad that goes with just about anything.

4 slices applewood-smoked bacon, chopped

½ cup buttermilk

¼ cup grapeseed oil

1 tablespoon lemon juice

½ teaspoon minced garlic

Kosher salt and coarsely ground black pepper

1 large fennel bulb with fronds

2 crisp apples, such as Gala or Jazz, cored and thinly sliced into half-moons

3 tablespoons chopped parsley

serves
-4-

Place the bacon in a cold medium skillet and cook over medium heat, stirring occasionally until crisp, about 10 minutes. Transfer to a paper-towel-lined plate to drain.

Meanwhile, in a blender, combine the buttermilk, oil, lemon juice, garlic, ½ teaspoon of salt and a few grinds of pepper; blend until smooth.

Cut the fronds from the fennel bulb; chop 2 tablespoons of fronds and set aside, discarding the remaining fronds (or reserve for making chicken stock). Quarter the fennel bulb and remove most of the core with a paring knife. Very thinly slice each fennel quarter lengthwise, preserving the pretty fan-like shape (a mandolin works best for this, but you can also use a knife).

Toss the fennel and apple with the buttermilk dressing in a large bowl and season with salt and pepper. Top with the parsley, fennel fronds and bacon and serve.

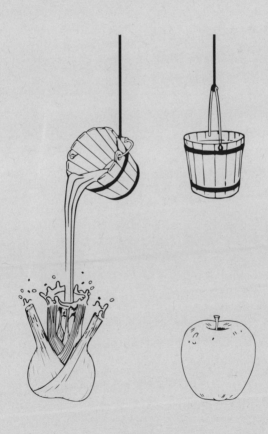

Spicy Apple Pickles

I am a pickle fanatic. At any given moment, my fridge will be stocked with three or four homemade variations and countless store-bought jars. Although I had never tasted an apple pickle before developing this recipe, I had a hunch that the fruit would be perfectly suited for preserving—and I was right. Bright and balanced, these pickles sing with lemony notes from the coriander and lemon zest and get a not-immodest kick from the arbol chiles. They pair perfectly with a platter of charcuterie and are also amazing on a *banh mi*.

---

6 dried arbol chiles

1 teaspoon coriander seeds

1½ cups unseasoned rice vinegar

3 tablespoons sugar

Kosher salt

makes 1 quart

2½ to 3 crisp apples, such as Granny Smith or Honeycrisp, cored and sliced into ¼-inch-thick half-moons

Two 2-inch-long strips lemon peel, removed with a vegetable peeler

In a small, dry skillet over medium heat, toast the chiles, turning occasionally, until they turn a shade darker, 1 to 2 minutes. Transfer to a plate to cool. In the same skillet, toast the coriander seeds until fragrant and a shade darker, 1 to 2 minutes; transfer to the plate.

Stem 3 of the chiles and grind them in a spice grinder with the coriander seeds until coarsely ground. Place them in a small saucepan and add the vinegar, 1 cup of water, the sugar and 2 teaspoons of salt. Bring to a simmer.

Meanwhile, place the apples, lemon zest and the remaining 3 whole chiles in a 1-quart jar. Add the simmering liquid to the jar and let cool, uncovered, to room temperature. Cover the jar and refrigerate overnight. The pickles can be refrigerated for up to 2 weeks.

Farro Pilaf with Pine Nuts

I love making grain salads with raw apple and knew that the combination of a nutty grain and a cooked, tender apple would go just as well together in a warm dish. This Mediterranean-inspired pilaf calls for pearled farro, which retains all the delicious flavor and texture of traditional farro, but cooks in half the time. The olive oil and spices bring out the savory side of the apple, revealing an almost vegetal quality that makes this dish a satisfying and versatile side dish with only a hint of sweetness.

serves 4

3 tablespoons extra-virgin olive oil

1 cup pearled farro

3 tablespoons pine nuts

½ small onion, finely chopped

1 cooking apple, such as Rome—cored, peeled and cut into ½-inch dice

¼ teaspoon crushed red pepper flakes

¼ teaspoon ground cumin

¼ teaspoon ground coriander

Large pinch ground allspice

Kosher salt and freshly ground black pepper

1 tablespoon chopped dill

Heat the oil in a medium saucepan over medium-high heat. Add the farro and pine nuts and cook, stirring, until lightly toasted, about 4 minutes. Add the onion and apple and cook, stirring, until slightly softened, about 2 minutes longer.

Add 1½ cups of water, the red pepper flakes, cumin, coriander, allspice, ½ teaspoon of salt and a few grinds of pepper. Bring to a boil, then reduce the heat to low and simmer, covered, until the liquid has been absorbed and the farro is tender but still toothsome, about 25 minutes. Let stand, covered, for 5 minutes.

Stir in the dill, season with salt and pepper to taste and serve.

Albin Family Thanksgiving Dressing

My family has been making this dressing every Thanksgiving for as long as I can remember. Buttery and rich (thanks to the challah) with sweet-tart little pockets of apple and prune and savory nuggets of celery and almonds, it strikes that perfectly addictive balance that keeps you going in for another bite. Don't substitute for the Granny Smiths here; you want that hit of acidity they contribute.

10 cups cubed challah bread (from a 1-pound loaf)

½ cup sliced almonds

1 stick unsalted butter

3 celery stalks, chopped

1 small onion, chopped

Kosher salt and freshly ground black pepper

3 Granny Smith apples—cored, peeled and cut into ½-inch pieces

1 cup pitted prunes, chopped

1 tablespoon chopped fresh thyme

1 tablespoon chopped fresh sage

1¾ cups turkey or chicken stock, preferably homemade

1 cup heavy cream

1 large egg, lightly beaten

serves
-8-

Preheat the oven to 300°. Spread the bread cubes on a baking sheet and bake until dried out, about 20 minutes. Transfer the bread cubes onto a plate and let cool. Increase the oven temperature to 375°. Spread the almonds on another baking sheet and bake until golden, about 6 minutes.

Melt the butter in a large skillet over medium heat. Add the celery, onion and ½ teaspoon of salt and cook, stirring occasionally, until softened, about 6 minutes. Add the apples and continue to cook, stirring occasionally, until the apples are almost tender, about 5 minutes. Stir in the prunes and herbs and transfer to a large bowl.

Add the bread, almonds, turkey stock, cream and ½ teaspoon of salt to the apple mixture and stir to combine; season with salt and pepper to taste, then stir the egg in thoroughly. Transfer to a 9-by-13-inch baking dish and cover tightly with foil. Bake the dressing until it is set in the center, about 45 minutes. Uncover and continue baking until the top of the dressing is golden brown, about 15 minutes longer. Serve alongside your holiday turkey.

Baked Apples Stuffed with Breakfast Sausage

If, like me, you can never decide between sweet and savory for brunch, consider making these sausage-stuffed apples to bridge the gap. If you have time, make the sausage mixture up to a day ahead; it will only improve the flavor. I love to serve these alongside fluffy buttermilk pancakes and douse the whole plate in maple syrup.

½ pound ground pork

2 tablespoons dried bread crumbs

2 tablespoons cold unsalted butter, cut into small bits

1 tablespoon pure maple syrup, plus more for drizzling

1 small garlic clove, finely grated

1 tablespoon minced fresh sage

1 teaspoon chopped fresh thyme

½ teaspoon freshly grated nutmeg

¼ teaspoon cayenne

Kosher salt and freshly ground black pepper

4 medium cooking apples, such as Braeburn

serves
-4-

Preheat the oven to 375°. In a bowl, mix the pork, bread crumbs, butter, 1 tablespoon of maple syrup, garlic, sage, thyme, nutmeg, cayenne, ¾ teaspoon of salt and ¼ teaspoon of pepper until very well combined.

Cut off the top third of each apple, reserving the tops and leaving the stem intact if there is one. Use a melon baller or measuring teaspoon to remove the core. Continue scooping out some of the apple flesh, leaving about ½-inch wall all around the inside of the apple. Chop up the scooped-out flesh and add it to the sausage mixture. Fill the apples with the sausage mixture, mounding it a bit above the rim of the apple and replace the top.

Nestle the apples in a small 1-quart baking dish or medium-size gratin dish and bake until the apples are tender and the sausage is fully cooked, about 55 minutes (an instant-read thermometer inserted into the center should register 160°). Drizzle with maple syrup and serve.

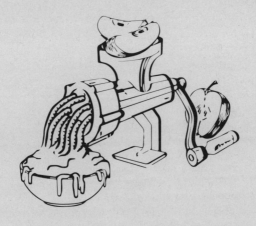

Pork Chops with Apple-Beet-Horseradish Compote

Sure, pork chops and applesauce are a classic combination, but this recipe amps up the apple component by brining the pork chops in homemade apple juice. The brine does double duty, not only adding flavor but also ensuring the chops stay moist and juicy. You'll be amazed by the incredible effect that even a quick 30-minute soak will have. The compote gets a modern update too; apples and beets share an earthy sweetness that makes them a natural pair in this piquant accompaniment.

5 crisp, sweet apples, such as Ambrosia, divided

3 tablespoons sugar, divided

Kosher salt and freshly ground black pepper

Four 1-inch-thick center cut bone-in pork chops (about 2½ pounds)

3 tablespoons unsalted butter

1 medium shallot, finely chopped

2 medium beets, peeled and cut into ½-inch cubes

1 tablespoon sugar

1 tablespoon fresh lemon juice

3 tablespoons prepared horseradish

2 tablespoons finely chopped chives

1 teaspoon apple pie spice

serves
·4·

Core and chop 2 of the apples. Add the apples to a blender along with 2 cups of water, 2 tablespoons of the sugar and 3 tablespoons of salt; puree until smooth. Pour the brine into a baking dish and add the pork chops, making sure they're submerged in the liquid. Refrigerate for at least 30 minutes and up to 4 hours.

Meanwhile, peel and core the 3 remaining apples and cut them into ½-inch cubes. Melt the butter in a medium saucepan over medium heat. Add the shallot and cook, stirring occasionally, until slightly softened, about 2 minutes. Add the beets and cook, stirring occasionally, until they begin to soften, about 8 minutes. Add the apples, ¼ cup of water and the remaining tablespoon of sugar and bring to a simmer. Cook, partially covered and stirring occasionally, until the liquid has thickened and the apples and beets are tender, about 10 minutes longer. Stir in the lemon juice and horseradish and season to taste with salt. Let stand until ready to serve (the compote can be served warm or at room temperature).

Preheat a grill to medium-high heat. Remove the pork chops from the brine and pat dry; season with the apple pie spice and a few grinds of pepper. Grill the pork chops until just cooked through but still pink in the center, about 5 minutes a side (an instant-read thermometer inserted into the center of the chop should register 140°). Let the chops rest for 5 minutes, then serve with the compote on the side.

Note: You can make your own apple pie spice blend by combining 2 parts ground cinnamon to 1 part each ground allspice and freshly grated nutmeg.

Barbecue Chicken with Asian Applesauce

This spicy barbecue sauce embodies the spirit of my hometown, Houston, which is an incredibly diverse and culturally rich city with culinary influences that span the globe. I grew up eating exceptional Vietnamese, Mexican and regional Texan cuisine there, and it forever influenced the way I eat and cook. This recipe marries those flavors into a bold sauce that unifies the bittersweet edge of caramel with the pungent kick of fish sauce, the smokiness of chipotle and the comforting flavor of applesauce.

2 cooking apples, such as Macintosh

⅓ cup apple cider vinegar

⅓ cup sugar

1 small yellow onion, finely chopped

3 garlic cloves, finely chopped

1 jalapeño pepper, chopped

3 tablespoons Asian fish sauce

1 tablespoon Sriracha

½ teaspoon chipotle powder

¼ cup chopped cilantro

Two 3½-pound chickens, cut into 6 pieces each

2 tablespoons vegetable oil

Kosher salt and freshly ground black pepper

serves 6 to 8

Grate the apples on the large holes of a box grater; transfer the pulp to a bowl and mix with the vinegar.

Place the sugar in a heavy-bottomed medium saucepan, add 1 tablespoon of water and mix until the mixture resembles wet sand. Heat the pan over medium-high heat and cook, undisturbed, until the sugar begins to melt. Continue cooking, swirling the pan occasionally, until all of the sugar has melted and the caramel is deep amber. Carefully add the onion, garlic and jalapeño and cook, stirring constantly, for 1 minute.

Stir in the apple-vinegar mixture, fish sauce, Sriracha, chipotle powder and ¾ cup of water. Simmer until the sauce is thickened and the apples are tender, about 20 minutes. Let the barbecue sauce cool slightly, then add the cilantro, transfer to a blender and puree until smooth.

Preheat a grill to medium heat. Toss the chicken with the oil and season lightly with salt and pepper. Place the chicken on the grill, skin side up. Cover the grill and cook, turning the chicken every 5 minutes, until it is partially cooked through, 25 minutes. At this point, begin basting the chicken with a thick coating of barbecue sauce, turning occasionally and basting more, until the chicken is fully cooked and the outside is glazed, about 15 minutes longer (an instant-read thermometer inserted into the center of the chicken should register 160°). Serve the chicken with your favorite barbecue accompaniments, such as coleslaw and potato salad.

Braised Country Ribs with Apple Sauerkraut

This rustic dish is perfect for those first truly cold days of autumn when the trees are almost bare and you begin to crave warm, satisfying braises. Country ribs, cut from the shoulder end of pork baby backs, are very meaty with few bones and have just the right amount of fat for a low, slow cook. Using hard cider as your cooking liquid boosts the apple flavor while helping to tenderize the pork.

---

2 pounds country pork ribs

Kosher salt and freshly ground black pepper

2 tablespoons vegetable oil

1 medium onion, sliced

1 pound sauerkraut, drained

3 crisp apples, such as Cameo—cored, peeled and sliced 1 inch thick

3 tablespoons all-purpose flour

One 12-ounce bottle hard apple cider

2 tablespoons light brown sugar

2 bay leaves

¼ teaspoon whole allspice berries

1 whole clove

2 tablespoons chopped dill

1 tablespoon apple cider vinegar

Sour cream, for serving

Crusty bread, for serving

serves
·4·

Season the ribs all over with salt and pepper. Heat the oil in a Dutch oven or large pot over medium-high heat and add the ribs in a single layer, taking care not to crowd them (you will have to work in batches). Sear the ribs on one side, about 2 minutes, then turn and continue cooking until all sides are nicely browned, about 6 minutes total per batch. Transfer the ribs to a plate and repeat with the remaining ribs.

Add the onion to the Dutch oven and cook, stirring, until golden, about 6 minutes. Add the sauerkraut and apples and sprinkle evenly with the flour. Stir to combine and cook for 1 minute. Add the hard cider, sugar, bay leaves, allspice, clove and ¼ teaspoon of salt. Return the ribs to the Dutch oven and stir so that they are coated in the sauerkraut mixture. Bring to a simmer, then reduce the heat to medium-low and cook, covered, at a bare simmer, until the pork is fork tender, 1½ to 2 hours. Stir in the dill and vinegar and season with salt and pepper. Serve in shallow bowls with a dollop of sour cream and crusty bread.

Apple-Bacon-Brie Tartines

Okay, so Brie and apple sandwiches are a little bit "retro," to be polite, but I don't care: They're delicious! These open-faced toasts have a lot of rich elements—Brie, bacon and, of course, onions caramelized in the bacon fat—so I use a tart apple to provide some contrast. And although I normally love strong cheeses; I like to remove the rinds of the Brie for this sandwich, as they can be a little harsh with the other flavors.

8 slices bacon

1 medium red onion, thinly sliced

1 tablespoon sugar

Kosher salt and freshly ground black pepper

1 tablespoon red wine vinegar

1 tart, crisp apple, such as Goldrush or Granny Smith

4 large slices sourdough bread, toasted

About 8 ounces ripe Brie, thinly sliced (rind removed, if desired)

serves
-4-

Place the bacon in a large, cold skillet, then cook over medium heat, turning occasionally, until crisp, 10 to 12 minutes; transfer to a paper-towel-lined plate to drain.

Pour off all but about 1 tablespoon of fat from the skillet. Add the onion, sugar and ¼ teaspoon of salt to the skillet and continue to cook over medium heat, stirring often, until the onions are tender and golden brown, about 20 minutes; stir in the vinegar.

Core and thinly slice the apple. Lay the bread out on a work surface and top evenly with the Brie. Break the bacon slices in half and lay them on top of the cheese, followed by the apples. Sprinkle lightly with salt and pepper, then top with the onions and serve.

Granny Smith and Celery Granita

There's no need to break out the ice cream maker every time you want a refined frozen treat. This delicately flavored granita is extremely easy to make and functions beautifully as a palate cleanser in an elegantly coursed meal or as a solo dessert on a hot summer day. The celery and apple flavors also go fabulously with tomato, so the granita can pivot toward savory dishes; try it as a refreshing accompaniment to a simple tomato salad.

4 Granny Smith apples, cored and roughly chopped

5 celery stalks, ends removed, chopped

2 tablespoons lemon juice

½ cup sugar

Fine salt

1 pinch ancho chile powder or cayenne

serves 4 to 6

In a blender, pulse the apples, celery, ½ cup of water, lemon juice, sugar, ¼ teaspoon of salt and ancho powder together into a fine pulp (work in batches if necessary). Transfer the mixture to a fine-mesh sieve set over a large bowl and press down on the solids with the back of a wooden spoon to squeeze out all of the juice. Discard the solids.

Pour the juice into an 8-by-8-inch metal baking dish and transfer to the freezer. When the mixture begins to freeze, after about 2 hours, begin scraping the ice with a fork every 30 minutes to break up the crystals. Continue freezing and scraping until the granita is completely frozen, with a fluffy, snow-like texture, 2 to 4 hours more. Scoop into small chilled glasses and serve.

Calvados Applesauce

Calvados is a brandy distilled from apples from the Lower Normandy region of France, and it makes a fitting backbone for this take on classic applesauce. Cooking the apples in the brandy imparts some of the spirit's caramel and vanilla aromas into the applesauce, and gives it a fuller, richer flavor that's further enhanced by the addition of butter. This dish is a departure from the snack of your youth; indeed, it's decadent enough to stand alone as dessert.

5 pounds cooking apples, such as Macintosh—peeled, cored and cut into ¾-inch cubes

¾ cup Calvados

1 tablespoon fresh lemon juice

2 tablespoons fresh orange juice

½ cup light brown sugar, plus more to taste if desired

4 tablespoons unsalted butter, cut into ½-inch pieces

1 teaspoon ground cinnamon

½ teaspoon pure vanilla extract

Preheat the oven to 350°. In a large bowl, toss all of the ingredients (except the vanilla) together and place them in a 4-quart glass or enamel baking dish. Cover tightly with foil and bake until the apples are very tender, about 1½ hours. Mash the apples thoroughly with a potato masher and stir in the vanilla. Add additional sugar to taste if desired. Cool completely. Serve the sauce any way you'd normally enjoy applesauce—as a snack, alongside pork chops or with a dollop of crème fraîche for dessert. The applesauce can be stored in an airtight container in the refrigerator for up to 1 week.

Gingered Apple Butter

Apple butter distills the flavor of apples down to their very essence; one taste can evoke the spirit of autumn in its entirety. My addition of ginger, in both fresh and powdered forms, elongates the seasonal charm of this dish with a new level of warmth and complexity. You can enjoy the butter in a number of ways, but I particularly love it on French toast.

4 pounds mixed apples, such as Cortland, Pink Lady and Braeburn—peeled, cored and chopped into ¾-inch cubes

2 cups apple cider

1 cup light brown sugar

One 2-inch piece fresh ginger, peeled and minced

3 tablespoons fresh lemon juice

½ teaspoon ground ginger

¼ teaspoon ground allspice

¼ teaspoon ground cinnamon

makes 2 cups

Preheat the oven to 300°. Combine all the ingredients in a Dutch oven and bring to a simmer over medium-high heat. Reduce the heat to medium and simmer, partially covered, until the apples are soft, about 25 minutes. Use an immersion blender to puree the apples (or puree in a blender in batches).

Transfer the Dutch oven, uncovered, to the oven. Bake, stirring every 20 minutes and scraping the bottom so that it does not burn, until the mixture is very thick and dark brown, 2 to 2½ hours. Cool completely, then transfer to an airtight container and refrigerate until ready to serve. The apple butter will keep for up to 1 week.

Apple Ring Fritters with Molasses Syrup

These sweet treats are like fluffy, tender cake doughnuts with a delicious soft apple center. Instead of seasoning the batter with typical partners such as cinnamon or allspice, I like to use Chinese five-spice powder, which includes star anise, clove, cinnamon, fennel seed and Sichuan peppercorn. The mixture hints at traditional baking spice flavors, but only slightly; the savory elements override the sugar with a hard-to-place warmth that makes these fritters really stand out. The molasses syrup pushes them over the top, but they're just as delicious dusted with powdered sugar.

⅓ cup molasses (not blackstrap)

Juice and finely grated zest of half an orange

¾ cup all-purpose flour

1 tablespoon sugar

1 teaspoon baking soda

½ teaspoon Chinese five-spice powder

Fine salt

1 large egg

½ cup whole milk

About 2 cups vegetable oil

3 crisp apples, such as Northern Spy or Granny Smith—peeled, cored and cut into ½-inch rings

serves
4 to 6

Combine the molasses, orange juice and zest in a small saucepan. Bring to a simmer over medium heat and simmer until slightly reduced, about 3 minutes.

Whisk the flour, sugar, baking soda, five-spice powder and a pinch of salt together in a medium bowl. In another bowl, whisk together the egg and milk. Add the milk mixture to the flour mixture and stir until just combined; the batter will be thick (be careful not to overmix).

Pour ½ inch of oil into a medium cast-iron skillet and heat it to 365° on a deep-fry thermometer over medium-high heat.

Coat the apple rings in the batter and fry, a few at a time, until golden brown and crisp, 2 to 3 minutes per batch. Transfer the rings to paper towels to drain. Return the oil temperature to 365° and repeat with the remaining apples. Serve the fritters with the molasses syrup.

Apple Tart with Tahini Frangipane

I was inspired to make this tart by my best friend, Manuela, who often eats apples with tahini as a snack. At first, I was unsure about the combination, but it turns out that the nutty, slightly bitter sesame paste goes amazingly well with apples and is leagues more interesting than the usual pairing with peanut butter. The fluffy, rich tahini frangipane tastes similar to halvah, which, combined with the orange flower water in the glaze, gives this tart a decidedly Middle Eastern bent.

For the dough:

1¼ cup all-purpose flour

2 tablespoons sugar

Fine sea salt

8 tablespoons cold unsalted butter, cut into ½-inch pieces

1 large egg yolk

½ teaspoon pure vanilla extract

3 tablespoons ice-cold water

For the filling:

6 tablespoons softened unsalted butter

1 cup sugar, plus more for sprinkling

¾ cup tahini

⅛ teaspoon pure almond extract

½ teaspoon pure vanilla extract

2 large eggs

3 tablespoons all-purpose flour

3 Granny Smith apples—peeled, cored and halved

1 tablespoon fresh lemon or orange juice

2 tablespoons apple jelly

1 teaspoon orange flower water

serves
•8•

Make the dough: Preheat the oven to 350°. In a food processor, pulse the flour, sugar and ⅛ teaspoon of salt together. Add the butter and pulse until the mixture resembles a course meal with some pea-size lumps. Add the egg yolk, vanilla and water and pulse until the mixture starts to form a dough. Turn out onto a floured surface and knead a few times just to bring the dough together. Transfer the dough to a 10-inch fluted tart pan with a removable bottom and press it out into an even layer over the bottom and up the sides; refrigerate until firm, about 20 minutes.

Line the crust with foil and fill with pie weights, dried beans or rice. Bake until the edge of the tart starts to turn golden, about 20 minutes. Remove the foil and pie weights and continue baking until the crust is golden all over, about 15 minutes longer. Transfer to a rack and let cool completely.

Meanwhile, make the filling: Beat the butter and sugar together in a large bowl with an electric mixer on high speed until light and fluffy, about 4 minutes. Add the tahini and extracts and beat until well combined. Add the eggs, one at a time, beating after each addition. Add the flour and beat until combined.

Scrape the frangipane into the tart shell and spread it evenly. Working with half an apple at a time, cut it crosswise into ¼-inch-thick wedges while holding the apple tightly to keep the cut pieces together. Press lightly on the apple to slightly fan the wedges, then transfer it (all together) onto the frangipane. Repeat with the remaining apples and arrange them on the surface in a circular pattern. Lightly brush the surface of the apples with the lemon or orange juice and sprinkle with a little sugar. Bake until the apples are tender and the frangipane is puffed and golden brown, about 1 hour. Transfer to a rack to cool.

In a small bowl, combine the apple jelly and orange flower water with ½ tablespoon of water and heat in the microwave until warm, about 30 seconds. Brush the mixture all over the surface of the apples. Let the tart cool completely before slicing and serving.

Apple & Dulce de Leche Tartlets

With just four ingredients and a total prep and cooking time of about 45 minutes, these gorgeous tarts are a bit of a miracle and definitely more than the sum of their parts. As the tarts bake, the puff pastry takes on a nutty, buttery flavor and the dulce de leche melds with the apples' juices, caramelizing and bubbling along the edges. Thin, flaky and alluringly golden, the finished product is impossible to resist.

One 14-ounce package frozen all-butter puff pastry, partially thawed

About ⅔ cup dulce de leche

2 crisp, sweet or tart apples, such as Jazz or Ambrosia

1½ tablespoons unsalted butter, cut into small bits

serves —4—

Preheat the oven to 400°. Line a baking sheet with foil.

Unfold the puff pastry and break or cut it into 4 equally sized rectangles. Arrange the rectangles on the prepared baking sheet and poke them all over with a fork. Warm the dulce de leche in the microwave until it's thin enough to pour, about 30 seconds. Drizzle each rectangle with 2 tablespoons of dulce de leche, making sure to leave a ½-inch border around the edges (reserve the remaining dulce de leche for drizzling at the end).

Peel the apples, then cut in half lengthwise and core them. Thinly slice each half crosswise and arrange half an apple on each tart so that the slices overlap slightly. Dot the tops of the apples evenly with the butter, then bake until the pastry is cooked through and golden brown, about 25 minutes. Transfer the tarts to a rack and drizzle with the remaining dulce de leche (rewarm in the microwave if necessary). Serve warm or at room temperature.

Apple-Olive Oil Cake

This cake occupies a heavenly middle ground between cake and custard. The olive oil and grated apple keep it exceedingly moist while giving it a subtle, sophisticated flavor best described as fruity and floral. The cake has a fairly high sugar content, but it's not overly sweet. Instead, the sugar helps create a delicious deep-golden crust around the cake. And best of all, this dessert only improves after a day or two.

1 cup extra-virgin olive oil, plus more for the pan

2 cups all-purpose flour

1¾ cups sugar

Fine sea salt

1 teaspoon baking powder

½ teaspoon baking soda

1 large sweet apple, such as Jazz, coarsely grated

⅓ cup apple juice or cider

¾ cup whole milk

3 large eggs

Lightly sweetened whipped cream for serving (optional)

serves
·8·

Preheat the oven to 350°. Lightly oil a 9-inch cake pan and line the bottom with parchment paper.

In a large bowl, whisk together the flour, sugar, 1 teaspoon of salt, baking powder and baking soda and set aside. In a medium bowl, whisk together the grated apple, apple juice, milk, eggs and the 1 cup of olive oil until very well combined. Add the wet ingredients to the dry and stir until incorporated. Pour the batter into the prepared cake pan and bake until the cake is deep-golden brown and the top of the cake springs back when touched, about 1 hour. Transfer to a wire rack and let the cake cool in the pan for 15 minutes, then remove from the pan and place on the rack to cool completely.

Serve the cake with lightly sweetened whipped cream, if desired.

Cheddar-Crusted Deep-Dish Apple Pie

This is not your grandma's apple pie, but it just might become your new family favorite. Without screaming cheese, the cheddar in the crust lends an added crispness and a savory quality that keeps you digging in for another bite. And the more fruity than peppery pink peppercorns bring an elegant note to the spicing in the filling. Still, this pie feels classic and would be at home on any holiday table.

For the crust:

2¾ cups all-purpose flour

Fine sea salt

10 tablespoons cold unsalted butter, cut into ½-inch pieces

2 cups shredded sharp yellow cheddar (about 8 ounces)

1 tablespoon apple cider vinegar

6 to 7 tablespoons ice-cold water

For the filling:

¾ cup sugar, divided, plus more for sprinkling on top

¼ teaspoon pink peppercorns, plus a little more for sprinkling on top

½ teaspoon ground cinnamon

4 pounds mixed apples, such as Gala, Pink Lady, Empire and Granny Smith

2 tablespoon apple cider vinegar

3 tablespoons all-purpose flour, plus more for dusting

2 tablespoons unsalted butter, cut into small bits

1 tablespoon whole milk or cream

serves
–8–

Make the crust: Combine the flour and 1 teaspoon of salt in a food processor and pulse to combine. Add the butter and pulse until the mixture resembles a course meal with some pea-size lumps of butter. Add the cheese and pulse to combine. Drizzle in the vinegar and 6 tablespoons of ice water. Pulse until the mixture starts to clump together. Squeeze some of the dough between your fingers; if it is too dry to stick together, add a little more cold water, ½ tablespoon at a time, until it does.

Turn half of the dough out onto a large piece of plastic wrap; gather it and knead a few times to bring it together. Form it into a disk and wrap well in plastic. Repeat with the remaining half of the dough. Refrigerate until firm, at least 1 hour and up to overnight.

Make the pie: Put a baking sheet in the center of the oven and preheat the oven to 425°. On a lightly floured surface, roll one disk of dough out into a 12-inch round. Ease it into a 9½-inch deep-dish pie plate and refrigerate.

Put ¼ cup of the sugar, the pink peppercorns and the cinnamon in a spice grinder or mini food processor and pulse until the peppercorns are very finely ground. Peel, core and thinly slice the apples (about ⅛ inch thick). Toss them in a bowl with the vinegar, the spiced sugar, the remaining ½ cup of sugar and the 3 tablespoons of flour. Mound the apples on top of the dough in the pie plate and dot with the butter. Roll out the second disk of dough to 12 inches and drape it over the apples, then crimp the top and bottom edges together to seal (trim any excess dough). Brush the top of the pie with the cream. Lightly crush a few pink peppercorns and sprinkle them on top, along with a little sugar. Using the tip of a sharp knife, cut 3 vents into the top of the pie.

Place the pie on the preheated baking sheet and bake for 20 minutes, then reduce the temperature to 375° and continue to bake until bubbling and golden brown, 35 to 40 minutes longer. Transfer to a rack and let cool completely before serving.

Apple Hot Toddy

In this autumnal riff on a hot toddy, you're essentially making a fast, fresh apple juice to use as your cocktail base. Brighter and less sweet than store-bought juice, it offers great apple flavor while still letting the bourbon shine through. Add the honey last so that you can tweak the warm cocktail to your preferred level of sweetness.

2 crisp apples, such as Jazz or Honeycrisp, cored and chopped

1 pinch ground cloves

½ cup bourbon

Juice of half a lemon (about 1 tablespoon)

3 to 4 tablespoons honey

4 cinnamon sticks for garnish (optional)

serves
·4·

Combine the apples, 2 cups of water and the cloves in a blender and puree until smooth. Strain through a fine-mesh sieve into a small saucepan; discard the solids. Add the bourbon and bring to a bare simmer over medium-high heat. Take the pan off the heat, stir in the lemon juice and add honey to taste. Serve in teacups with cinnamon sticks, if desired.

Apple- & Shiso-Infused Sake

Infusing sake with apples amplifies the rice-based wine's fruity aroma and adds a bit of sweetness and depth to the flavor, while the shiso contributes a subtle herbal note. Serving the drink over ice dilutes it ever so slightly and allows the flavors to blossom. This refreshing cocktail pairs extremely well with ceviche and other delicately prepared fish.

One 720 to 730 milliliter bottle dry sake (about 3 cups)

2 crisp apples, such as Fuji or Pink Lady, cored and cut into matchsticks

5 shiso leaves or ¼ cup mixed mint and basil leaves

A few dashes lemon or orange bitters

serves
-6-

Combine the sake, apples and shiso in a pitcher or large jar. Cover with plastic wrap or a lid and refrigerate, stirring occasionally, at least 24 hours and up to 2 days. Serve over ice with some of the apple and a dash of bitters.

Thank You!

Thanks to my husband, Jeff, for helping me make every recipe the best that it could be and for eating nothing but apple dishes for days on end. Thanks to my parents, Jorge and Veronica, for instilling in me the love of food and cooking. Thanks to my BFF, Manuela, for our daily chats and lots of feedback. Thanks to my kitty, Rascal, for walking all over the kitchen counter and constantly getting in my way. And thanks to everyone at Short Stack Editions for being so awesome!

—Andrea Albin

Share your Short Stack cooking experiences with us (or just keep in touch) via:

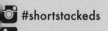 #shortstackeds 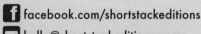 facebook.com/shortstackeditions
@shortstackeds hello@shortstackeditions.com

Colophon

This edition of Short Stack was printed by Circle Press in New York City on Neenah Astrobrights Lunar Blue (interior) and Neenah Oxford White (cover) paper. The main text of the book is set in Futura and Jensen Pro, and the headlines are set in Lobster.

Sewn by: *EEJ*

Available now at ShortStackEditions.com:

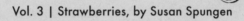
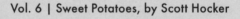
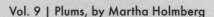